Journey Through Thistles & Time

Journey Through Thistles & Time

(2nd in the Humbler Poet Series)

by

Joan Tenner

Journey Through Thistles & Time

Published by Wisdom House Books, Inc.
Chapel Hill, North Carolina 27517 USA
www.wisdomhousebooks.com

Wisdom House Books is committed to excellence in the publishing industry.

Book design copyright © 2023 by Wisdom House Books, Inc. All rights reserved.

Cover and Interior Design by Ted Ruybal

Published in the United States of America

Hardcover ISBN: 978-1-7332444-3-5
Paperback ISBN: 978-1-7332444-5-9
LCCN: 2023907393

1. POE023000 | POETRY: Subject & Themes - General
2. POE023050 | POETRY: Subject & Themes - Family
3. LCO022010 | LITERARY COLLECTIONS: Subject & Themes General

First Edition 1984 | Second Edition 2023

25 24 23 22 21 20 / 10 9 8 7 6 5 4 3 2=

This book is dedicated to my mother, Elizabeth Schneider, and to my husband, Tom, whose love and camaraderie made her last years bearable.

Table of Contents

My Necessity 1

When Someone's Listening 2

By Direction 3

I Had to Let Her Go 4

All Things Decreed 5

Fate! Fact? 6

Magic Soup 7

Our First Christmas Tree 8

"Grandma, What Are These?" 10

Nonsense in the Nursery 11

Letter to Ashley 14

Leftovers from Thanksgiving 15

Folks Who Don't Exist 16

Poor Gray Mouse 18

Spider and Me 19

Phones in Heaven? 21

Saga of Rebel Ant 23

A Valid Correlation 26

Driftwood Friends 28

The Boat Ride 29

Bermudian Lullaby 30

Secrets 'twixt Us Three 32

To Face the Storm 33

It's Over 35

Now! 36

The Assault of Winter 37

Disillusion 39

Somber Landscape 41

What You Can Do 42
Say "This is False Prophecy" 43
World! Shame on You 45
Search for Misplaced Treasure! 47
Always Near By 49
Folded linens 51
Acceptance 52
Somewhere 53
Until Then 54
Reprimand 55
Lost 56
The Struggle 57
Exhausted! 58
To Sleep 59
Optimistic Me! 60
On a Hot Afternoon 61
More Like a Bird 63
The Couch is Mine 65
A Hodgepodge 67
Neither Less—Nor More 68
There's No Excuse 70
Double Trouble 71
Bounty in Winter 72
What's Next? 73
It's Time to Move-On 74
The Face of Reality 76
Prayer for Winnie 77
A Variable Constant 78
Prenatal, Again 79
The Host 80
The Leaving 81

The thistle plant has deep roots and can flourish even in very poor soil. Its flowers are beautiful but almost impossible to gather. Because of its "barbs" it is seldom touched. In many ways, life's journey is like a thistle—beautiful to behold but painful to grasp.

Most of these poems were written to make you laugh, cry, remember, bring you solace and/or inspiration. A few of them are intended to "prick" the conscience of society on certain issues that are also deep rooted and seldom touched.

Come, journey with me, through thistles and time.

My Necessity

Today is a day that's all my own!
I've reserved it just for me!
I'll lock the door, unplug the phone,
And make a pot of tea.

Music locked on records
Will come alive today!
Books that do not speak a word
Will have so much to say!

There'll be time to read old letters
Or to write a poem or two,
Time to sew on buttons
Or to polish dusty shoes.

The world shut out, and I shut in,
Is effective therapy.
I pluck the thistles from my soul
When I take time for me.

When Someone's Listening

A songbird's in the meadow
Waiting to be heard,
Hoping she can sing as well
As any other bird.

She has not the look of beauty
And her notes may not be pure,
But there's feeling and emotion
In her chirping overture.

Let the song bird sing.
Listen with your heart.
Weigh each warbling note
And chirping counterpart.

Every bird is some bird
And every bird must sing.
Each song will much the sweeter be
When someone's listening.

By Direction

Step to the music!
You cannot quell the surge
Of lullaby, wedding march or dirge,
Nor fake defection.

Step to the music!
Though you be still, you dance.
The music plays, not by chance
But by direction.

I Had to Let Her Go

It was a life too transient
(too fragile to remain),
A rare exquisite being
That will never live again.

I prayed to stay existence!
They said she would not live.
I gave her birth to realize
Life was not mine to give.

Curse you! Willful wings of time!
I begged that you might drift
(This once) to slow thy flight.
You were exact and swift.

In the land of all that's holy,
I pray her soul will know:
I had not the power to hold her,
And I had to let her go.

All Things Decreed

Persuaded by a gentle breeze,
A pine cone fell beneath the tree
On which it formed, long months before.

When the tender, warming sun
Coaxed the pine cone open wide,
It loosed the seeds once trapped inside,
Because their time had come.

The purpose of the cone fulfilled,
It lay decaying in the rains
That sweetly suckled and sustained
The sapling trees the seeds became,
Because their time had come.

The cycle constantly repeats,
From tree to cone to seed to tree.
So it goes with you and me
Through birth and death and destiny,
Because our time has come.

From beneath the sea to the rims of space,
And beyond to other galaxies,
In cycles planned from eternity,
All things decreed to be—
Will be—when their time has come.

Fate! Fact?

We are born
Unaware of the event.

Without choice
We accept our countenance.

We wrap ourselves in dreams
To endure reality.

We exist and toil
Uncertain in our purpose.

We meet death
Without an introduction.

Will we not find heaven
Without searching for it?

Magic Soup

I've tasted many kinds of soup,
Made on my kitchen floor
By tiny chefs with wooden spoons
And pots and pans galore.

A pinch of this, a bit of that,
So sweetly were they blended
By little hands that measured
The ingredients, pretended.

"Taste it, Mommy. It is good!"
My little ones would say.
I sipped on that supreme cuisine
So many times each day!

What innocence is make believe!
The soup was judged "delicious"
So naturally, we ate it
From imaginary dishes.

Long years have passed since I have sipped
Such savory soup as then.
Now my grandchild's in the kitchen,
And it's soup time once again!

A Grandmother's delight

Our First Christmas Tree

Bring the boxes from the attic!
It's time to trim the tree.
Gather 'round! There's lots to do
For all the family.

Each ornament, in tissue stored
So carefully last year
Will speak a lot of memories
Of times and friends held dear.

We bought this one for our first tree,
Quite small but elegant.
One string of lights was all we had
And six small ornaments.

The tree stood in a bucket,
Wedged solidly with books
The ornaments were hung in front
With paper clips for hooks.

We bought a box of tinsel
Which only cost a dime,
And so it was we trimmed the tree
One sliver at a time.

The sparse lit tree reflected light
From every tinsel strand!
How was it possible to be
So small and yet so grand?

"Our First Christmas Tree" continues . . .

Then Santa (for our children,
As each Christmas came and went)
Added many strings of lights
And scores of ornaments.

Now, each trinket is a treasure
Relating to the past
And each Christmas tree is larger
And more splendid than the last!

Still, our first tree was the finest!
None since cast such a spell!
So small a tree—so small—yet we
Remember it so well.

"Grandma, What Are These?"

"Grandma, what are these?"
Small fingers traced
The veins on the back of my hand.
I said, "That's—that's—Grandma's getting old."
(She was too young to understand.)

"When I grow old
I won't have these",
Said she, convincingly,
Then shook her head
In sweet denial
When I said, "Wait and see."

It is my prayer
That life will gift
To her—the same as me,
To one day feel
Small fingers question:
"Grandma, what are these?"

Nonsense in the Nursery

Mistress Mary, quite contrary,
How does your garden grow?
I know it's none of my business,
But I'd really like to know!

Jack Sprat could eat no fat.
His wife would eat not lean.
They changed to vegetarian
And both ate mustard greens.

Jack and Jill went up the hill
To fetch old Mother Goose.
They both fell down and wonder still
"How did that goose get loose?"

Jack be nimble!
Jack be quick!
Somebody stole the candlestick!

Humpty Dumpty sat on a wall.
He held on tight so he wouldn't fall.
All the king's horses and men stayed away.
'cause an egg gets rotten in the sun all day!

"Nonsense in the Nursery" continues . . .

Little Bo Peep has lost her sheep
And doesn't want to find them.
Leave her alone! She wants to stay home,
And have her brothers mind them.

🐾

Little Jack Horner sat in a corner.
His teacher put him there.
His Christmas pie got squashed because
He put in on teacher's chair.

🐾

Little Boy Blue, come blow your horn.
The sheep in the meadow are all forlorn!
The mistress is making a dreadful sound.
The needle in the haystacks just been found!

🐾

Baa baa Black Sheep
Have you any wool?
Where have you stashed
Your three bags full?
Did you give it to your mistress?
Did you give it to your dame?
You look a bit sheepish
Stark naked in the lane!

🐾

Hey, Diddle Diddle, the cat and the fiddle
The cow jumped over the moon!
To be perfectly candid, she winced as she landed.
It's a long way down from the moon!

🐾

"Nonsense in the Nursery" continues . . .

There was a little girl
Who had a little curl;
The rest of her hair straight.
She fussed and she moaned
And brushed and combed,
And for every date—she was late.

Four and twenty blackbirds
Were baked up in a pie.
When the pie was opened
They could no longer sing!
Their feathers saved the baker's neck
By tickling the king.

Little Miss Muffet
Sat on a tuffet
Counting her curds
And weighing her whey.
Because she did pity
A poor hungry kitty
She gave all her whey away.

Letter to Ashley

Dear Ashley,

I think of you so frequently!
I study your picture and love to see
Your cherub face as it smiles at me.

Sometimes, just for a little while,
My imagination and will beguile
Your presence right out of the frame
On to my lap, and I whisper your name
And I hug you so hard!

I kiss your fingers and little nose
And admire the shoes that warm your toes.
You giggle and wiggle and touch my face
And my heart is so choked by your tight embrace!
I can hardly breathe!

Grandmas are not always privileged to be
Living nearby, though they'd like to be.
I'm writing this letter so you will know
When you're all grown up, that I loved you so!

BY JOAN TENNER

Leftovers from Thanksgiving

The love I hold for holidays
Is due, at least, in part
To the memories of each
Stored within my heart.
The smell of roasting turkey
Enjoyed Thanksgiving Day
Is the same, yet not the same
On any other day.
That which alters the aroma,
Re-living by-gone pleasantries
Brings flavors to perfection.
This nostalgic potpourri
Concocted from the past
Makes the feast so special
With leftovers that last!

Folks Who Don't Exist

Symbolic folks, whom we all know,
Are *timely* folks. They come and go.
They never wished for worldly fame,
Yet everybody knows their names!

We all know well of Father Time.
At half past May, he's in his prime.
He starts to age in late September,
Bent and bearded come December,
With scythe and glass of sand, he'll stay
Till New Year's Eve, then sneak away.
Amid the cheers and hugs and tears,
A diapered infant then appears.
Symbolic (as the baby is,
Time was too old, it can't be his)
It represents the brand new year
And stays one day, then disappears!

Now if you try you well might name
A dozen others of such fame.

Consider folks like Uncle Sam,
A country's image, not a man.
Jack Frost, who symbolizes cold,
Blows icy breath around the world.
Three Ice Men Days arrive in May.
The Man in the Moon is there to stay.
Mother Nature holds the key
To Mother Earth's menagerie.
With magic dust, the Sandman comes
To hasten sleep for little ones.

"Folks Who Don't Exist" continues . . .

There is nothing you can't do
When Lady Luck abides with you.
I never knew (till I made this list)
So many folks who don't exist!

Poor Gray Mouse!

Nibble, nibble, little gray mouse!
We don't want you in our house.
If you'd just leave the way you came,
There'd be no need to play this game!

Our house is large, but we can't share,
For, though you're small, you're quite a scare!
The traps are set, poor little mouse.
Too bad you came into our house!

I hope your sibling mice will stay
Out in the fields where they can play.
Nibble, nibble, poor gray mouse.
You cannot live here in my house.

Spider and Me

I caught a lovely butterfly
And put him in a jar.
I thought I'd let him rest a while.
He must have traveled far!

The next day when I went to see
My friend the butterfly,
He wasn't moving any more
And I began to cry.

My mother said the butterfly
Should never have been jarred.
He would have been a friend for me
To play with, in our yard.

The flowers there like butterflies
And do not mind a bit
When fussy little butterflies
Upon their blossoms sit.

Now I just watch the butterflies
And never, never touch.
I tell them, when they visit me
"I love them very much!"

I caught a spider in a jar,
And through the glass, I watched him.
He looked so lonely and so scared
It made me sad I'd caught him.

"Spider and Me" continues . . .

I knew I'd have to let him go.
I hoped he wouldn't bite me.
I cocked the lid. He ran away!
He didn't even like me.

Spiders aren't like butterflies
He never came again.
I think I must have scared him
And he must have told his friends.

My mother and my daddy said
I shouldn't feel so bad.
"Spiders never make good friends."
Still, I felt very sad.

So, I just played with butterflies
Until my birthday came,
When Daddy gave me a surprise!
Spider was his name!

My daddy brought a great big box
And gave it carefully.
The cutest little puppy dog
Jumped out and barked at me!

The weather changed and it's too cold
For butterflies to come,
But we don't even miss them.
We're having so much fun!

My puppy isn't scared of me,
And he can't fly away,
And I can't put him in a jar.
So we are friends, to stay!

BY JOAN TENNER

Phones in Heaven?

Let me tell you of a dream—A silly dream
I won't forget!
I'd eaten too much cake and cream
And went to bed a bit upset.

I dreamed that I lay dying!
A phone rang close to my bed.
It was all I could do to answer it.
"You've got the wrong number," I said.

It soon rang again. From my coma I woke,
Mumbled an oath, in my agony, spoke:
"I'm dying. I don't need a thing
Except a phone that will not ring!"

As I expired, the phone rang again.
"This is Peter," insisted a voice.
"Before you may enter our heavenly center
You must answer our survey of choice."

"Not now," I said. "Just find me a bed
In a room with no telephone.
With pure peace and quiet and adequate diet,
I'll be happy to call this my home."

But Peter continued his long questionnaire:
"Gold or silver shoes? Soft drinks or booze?
Sheets—satin or silk? Coffee, tea or milk?
We will order whatever you choose."

"Phones in Heaven?" continues . . .

"I thought," said I, with an angry sigh,
"You could read my thoughts and you'd know!"
Pete could tell I was riled. He said, with a smile,
"There is some place else you can go!"

So I calmed myself, took Pete by the arm,
Said, "I'm sorry old boy. I was rude."
"No shoes—booze—silk—milk
Now, I'd like to be shown to my room.

Then Pete let me in, and to my chagrin,
As I looked down that long golden street,
I saw telephone lines and high wooden poles
Anchored in golden concrete!

A phone rang again, and rang and rang
Till I found myself awake.
I was too befuddled to answer it.
I had had all the calls I could take!

Now every time my telephone rings
I think about this dream.
It all goes to show how little I know
About heaven, (and cake and cream).

This is a very *phoney* tale,
However fun to write!
I apologize to Saint Peter.
Dis-reverence isn't right!

Saga of Rebel Ant

I heard a sad story a short time ago
Of a hard working ant who wished to go
To see the world he had never known,
So he packed his sack and left his home.

Out of the anthill into the light
Emerged an ant who knew no fright!
To avoid those creatures who'd gobble him up,
He slept in the blossom of a buttercup.

He would dine at leisure on whatever he'd find,
Then relax on the fuzz of the cucumber vine.
He was ever so happy! His life was sublime!
This world was so lush in the summertime!

After a while, he felt strangely alone.
His thoughts kept wandering back to his home.
He scampered about and tried to pretend
That he wasn't alone—that he had a friend.

As the summer days passed, his loneliness grew.
He longed for his folks and friends that he knew.
Loneliness proved so depressing a state
That he vowed to go home, no matter his fate.

Back to the anthill he traveled that day.
He would always remember his leisure and play,
But he made up his mind to swallow his pride,
And promised to work, so they let him inside.

"Saga of Rebel Ant" continues . . .

"Come in," said the Queen with no welcoming smile.
"You're back," she said, "in time for your trial."
"You sere selfish and lazy not to have stayed!
There would be no anthill if everyone played."

"The faithful workers who stayed at home
Had to do your chores, as well as their own.
You are *ant-i-social!* You are guilty of neglect!
You are no longer fit to be called an insect!"

"Your sentence must be as great as your crime.
Henceforth, you will spend all of your time
Defending the hill against enemy spiders,
Who threaten our home and all its insiders."

"Be brave and be clever. If you succeed,
By proving your worth, you'll atone for your deed."
That seemed to be fair, so the rebel ant went
To battle the foes of the settlement!

This brave little ant who knew no fright
Gallantly fought with all of his might!
In spite of his valor, he didn't last long.
By giving his life, he righted his wrong.

The spiders were many! They picked the hill clean.
They scrambled her eggs and devoured the Queen.
Not one ant was left—to work or to play.
The whole hill had crumbled that terrible day.

I've thought about this story.
I must admit my sympathy
Goes to every ant who lived
in that community.

"Saga of Rebel Ant" continues . . .

Still, I must contend
that Rebel Ant was not all bad!
I think he had more courage
than the other ants had!

It wasn't that he minded
all the work he had to do.
He simply had the notion
that the world held pleasures, too.

I can't imagine living
Just to work, day after day!
I'm glad I wasn't born an ant!
I too, would run away!

A Valid Correlation

"Bad dog!" I scolded.
"You've dirtied the floor!"
"Must you always dig
when you're let out of doors?"
He whined, and with sad eyes looked up.
"Why won't you learn, you ungrateful pup?"
His great dark eyes admitted guilt.
He looked so cute with head atilt!

"You're not bad," I said.
"You don't mean to upset me.
In time, you will learn
to love and respect me.

Then I tightly hugged him and suddenly
I thought about God and how He forgives me.
I wondered about how the Lord sees us—
Perhaps, akin to this untrained pup?

He cares for us
with such gentle compassion!
He knows how fragile
and weak we are fashioned.
We are sweet, amusing, unknowing at birth.
Like the puppy, we have to grow into worth.
We look up, hoping that He will forgive
Each time we transgress as we learn to live.

"A Valid Correlation" continues . . .

He probably says in a loving way,
Just what I said to my puppy today:
"You're not bad. You don't mean to upset me.
In time, you will learn to love and respect me."

This correlation seems valid, you see,
For God is the Master and I am just me.

Driftwood Friends

As the sea and palms were forced to dance
By a gusty wind, we met by chance,
Four souls on a darkened beach.

We recognized a kinship there
Which might have gone unnoticed where
Daylight blinds intuitive reach.

When Magdalene wiped His face with a cloth-
When Simon helped to carry His cross-
Each found their reason for being!

What purpose our meeting may never be known.
Providence gives many gifts to His own.
We accept, with profound thanksgiving.

The Boat Ride

Translucent puffs of moon-lit cotton
decorate the skies.
Reflected lights on ebon water
tend to hypnotize.
Sparkling ripples seem to spread
beyond infinity.
We revel in this ambiance of
pure tranquility.
Mesmerized, our arms entwine,
our spirits join, we kiss.
Heaven must be made of moments
comparable to this!

We melt—into the splendor of it all!

Bermudian Lullaby

In a blanket of blue,
her mother, the sea
Cradles Bermuda
so lovingly!
Softly the blanket
ripples and folds,
Kissing the shore
with repeated rolls.
A lullaby of
constant motion
Amuses the two,
Island and Ocean

Though green are her hills
all speckled with flowers,
And peaceful her pace,
restful the hours
That pass
in playful harmony
'tween child and mother,
island and Sea—
Beneath her mother's
protective lap
Lies a treacherous,
dangerous, beckoning trap!

The reefs and the shoals
keep intruders away.
Most uncharted, unbidden
ships go astray.
She claws at their hulls

"Bermudian Lullaby" continues . . .

and crushes their sides,
Then sucks them below
with her swirling tides!
Our's to reason,
when the ocean goes wild,
She is merely a mother
protecting her child."

Oh Sailor, come softly
to this lovely isle!
Chart well thy course,
and pray thee the while
You infringe on her blanket,
deceivingly soft.
Keep watch from your crow's nest!
Keep all hands aloft!
Sail true to thy course
and deviate not
If you would be spared
from the grave water lot.

Hundreds of hulls lie
locked in her coral,
Their treasures now crusted
with salt water spoil.
You can hear
if you listen attentively,
Mixed with the roar
of the open sea,
The moaning of sailors
who haunt the debris,
All part of that lullaby,
sung endlessly
To Bermuda,
Exquisite child of the sea!

Secrets 'Twixt Us Three

It's after midnight—almost one.
The duties of the day are done.
The usual boring day—today—
In its usual boring way—is over.

I cringe as I look in the mirror . . .
Gray, bent, wrinkled, spent.
I cannot ascertain what is wrong!
Life is so changed
When there is no song.
The days are dull and long.

I need this time to think,
To empty my soul
Of recycling guilt—
To regain control!
I shall be pleased
To shed this shroud.
I cannot, with ease,
Say this aloud.

So, I bond my thoughts to paper,
Secrets ' twixt us three.
Never were three friend so close
As paper, pen and me.

To Face the Storm

I hear a subtle
Whisper of a wind!
An inevitable storm
Will soon begin.
It will intensify
In strength
To such a power,
Pitch and length
As to do the worst!

Till now, I managed
To restrain it,
By vigilance
Contained it,
By determination
Chained it.
(Perhaps that was my error.)
I feel the chill!
I taste the terror!
Events are out of my control.
I am weary, heart and soul.

What now? My task—
To face the storm,
To watch it build
And let it ravage,
Intractable and savage.
It cannot be denied.
There is no place to hide!

"To Face the Storm" continues . . .

The storm will split and splinter
'til it's spent.
What it does not shatter
Will be bent.
If I survive,
My world could be quite changed.
There will be matters
Of the heart to rearrange.

I knew a storm was certain
But not when.
Enough to trust
There will be calm again.

It's Over!

The storm has calmed,
Leaving cloudy thoughts
And drenched emotions.
A warming balm
Of forgiving arms
Restores our unity
And leaves us wondering:
What brought
The storm about?

Now!

Be aware
Of sounds,
Of silence,
Sunsets,
Love,
Even pain!

After life,
Such as these
Will not have been
Nor come again.

The Assault of Winter

Under gray and heavy skies
A swift wind whirls, and swirls
The chimney's dark designs
Into dissipating curls.
It blows the falling snow
To powder Nature's weary face,
Changing faded colors
Into reflective grace.

Nature rests. Pregnant with
The bounty of God's earth,
She nurtures every seed
Toward its scheduled birth.
The animals and birds
Are considerately quiet
As they forage and consume
Their meager winter diet.

Bent branches hand inverted,
And pretty patterns make.
The forests labor silently
Beneath the icy weight.
Farmstead windows glow with frost
And dance with specks of light.
The backs that ached at harvest
Now rest in snug delight.

While warring Winter trumpets
Frigid fanfares' cross the range,
He knows his days are numbered.
He knows, but will not change

"The Assault of Winter" continues . . .

Until his fortress crumbles
Beneath the mighty sun
That warms the way for Spring
When Winter's days are done.

Though his assault be bitter,
Winter never ever wins.
Nature waits and bides the time
Until the thaw begins.
Protected progeny of
Every species yet survives
And will reclaim the earth
When gentle Spring arrives.

Disillusion

Thirty years had passed and then,
I wanted to go home again.
I took my winter-holiday,
Some extra clothes and two weeks' pay,
And presently was on my way
On rails that sped to yesterday.

The train was old. The seats were torn.
Those still intact were badly worn.
I could recall when it was new.
Proudly polished by a crew,
It carried milk and mail and made
Deliveries to the local trade.

I spent long hours on the train
With memories tumbling in my brain
I heard the porter call my town
And felt the train was slowing down—
Grabbed my grip and disembarked,
Excitement pounding in my heart!

The train continued on its way.
I searched to find a place to stay.
I walked the streets where once I'd known
The shape of every cobblestone,
Where once I played so happily,
Where every home was known to me.

The parlor lights that once did glow
And warm the panes of each window
Had disappeared, and as I feared,

"Disillusion" continues . . .

Some homes had not survived the years.
I closed my eyes. The wind blew cold.
We had grown distant, growing old.

The town and I were strangers, now.
It seemed impossible, somehow!
There used to be an Oak tree here!
We built our tree-house every year,
In June, when books were laid away.
It was our favorite place to play.

There in the lofty tree-house shade
We'd lunch on bread and marmalade.
We'd quench our thirst with lemonade.
Or root beer, that our mamas made.
The Oak was gone and weeds grew 'round
A rotted stump that hugged the ground.

I walked across the promenade
To find the squares were cracked and frayed.
It suddenly occurred to me:
"The past is best in memory!"
I ran to catch the midnight train
And vowed not to return again.

I soon returned to reality.
The present, I learned, is the place to be.
Although there exists nostalgia when
My memory takes me home again,
Today and all of the days ahead
Are still alive. The past is dead.

Somber Landscape

Along a modern Texas highway
Near an old abandoned town,
There's a somber piece of landscape
Overlooked and overgrown.

Where
        rain-stained statues
        stare
        at wind torn gates,
        and crooked crosses
        kneel
        on sunken mounds.

Where
        marble markers
        prove
        the rub of time,
        and vines bind
        rusty fences
        to the ground.

Where
        no one comes
        and no one cares,
        and few remember
        who rests where,
        (like the town)
        abandoned there.

Where
        life's components
        to elements
        decay.
        Where time and matter
        blend
        and, like the landscape,
        fade away.

What You Can Do

Don't envy the philosopher
His lofty, brilliant mind.
None has yet convinced the world
Of truth of any kind!

If truth be known by each of us,
Still we would difference know.
What one reasons to believe,
To him, is truth (as truth be so).

Believe as you will, whatever!
It is your privilege: your decision.
Waste not a moment of your life
In argument or derision.

Determine to bury bigotry
In the muck of its own disgrace,
Then witness the world's metamorphosis
To a peaceful and beautiful place.

Say "This is False Prophecy"

Once, ere mankind had evolved,
The virgin earth, serene, revolved
Unscathed by caustic recrement,
Tranquil in its years of advent,
Green of land and blue of skies.
Indeed, it was a paradise!
So pure, so pleasing, the Creator
Deemed to share what He had made.
He sculpted His envisaged "man"
Who multiplied at His command.
How beautifully it all began!

Now, urban orges crowd the sky.
Bold and gaudy buildings high,
Stacked with brick and steel and shutter
Form a mortared maze of clutter,
Those who hold to large domain,
Squeeze the symbol coin of gain
In grisly greed. They will not share;
While hunger hovels everywhere
Grotesque in consequence!

From the crowded ghetto, where
Starving ashen faces stare,
Thunderous moans of deprivations
Drum a warning to all nations
With all of hell's intensity!
"An equalizing destiny,
Shaped within a mushroom cloud
Will cremate humble with the proud!"

"Say 'This is False Prophecy'" continues . . .

Oh! Say this is false prophecy!
Say it need not—will not be!
Say that brotherhood will spread.
Say the hungry will be fed!
Say—Nostradamus saw in error!
Say we need not live in terror.
Pray that tolerance will grow.
All must strive to make it so.
Each must try to understand
The needs of every child of man,
Or—what most we fear—will be!

World! Shame on You!

Not financially able,
(Too costly the load)
Can't two women share
A platonic abode?

Or two men do the same
Without living in fear
Of acquiring the name
Of a gay or queer.

Or a man and a women,
To comfort each other,
Share late lonely years
As sister and brother?

How quickly we judge!
How cruel our contention!
Without fact or truth
We debase their intentions.

A display of affection
One man to another,
Is labeled as strange
And brands each as "lover."

Such love is too risky!
You are branded as odd.
We no longer reserve
Judgments to God.

"World! Shame on You!" continues . . .

We accuse them of sin.
We surmise and suppose.
We harass and condemn,
Though God alone knows!

Sad is the world
That must not display
Any love for another
For what others might say!

In self-righteous scrutiny
We decry what others do.
Which alters love to apathy
 World! Shame on you!

Search for Misplaced Treasure!

She cannot explain
Why she feels as she does.
He looks for the reason
she no longer loves
In the more tender ways
of their yesterdays.

He tries to hold her.
She shrinks away.
He does not understand.
She does not say
"The core of her love
has been chipped away."

So many frustrations
have altered her heart.
Trite altercations
have torn it apart.
She can't get her feelings
together again.

Their lives seem so changed;
but love is not dead.
What once was ambrosia
has turned into bread.
She takes no delight
in sharing his bed.

There is no warmth,
not even a kiss.
Neither is happy
with love amiss.

"Searching for Misplaced Treasures!" continues . . .

So many marriages
end like this.

"Who's fault?" You may ask.
Neither and both.
It's a long way back
to the marriage oath!
Love's ways are strange.
People change.

Each needs to search
for the treasure lost.
Repair it, restore it,
whatever the cost.
While both yet live,
both can forgive.

Each must go back
to when love was alive.
Go all the way back
to the groom and the bride.
Search hand in hand
and side by side.

If they can find
where they drifted apart,
Forget what came after
and make a new start,
They will face cold December
with June in their hearts.

In those late years (most vulnerable)
when the world seems not to care,
Old age may alter passion
but if tenderness is there,
The treasury of love and life
yet holds choice gifts to share!

BY JOAN TENNER

Always Near By

I couldn't help hearing this tearful lament
From a son to his mother. The monologue went:

"Mother, I've come to your grave today,
'cause I wasn't here when you went away.
I'm so ashamed and I miss you so!
I should have come home a long time ago.

Mother, please tell me what to do!
I want your forgiveness and I need you.
I wish I could tell you how much I have learned.
I thought that you'd be here when I returned.

Mother, I hope you are listening.
I truly regret my wandering.
I'm sorry for all that I didn't do.
I should have stayed here to care for you.

Somehow, I know that you'd understand
If I could just see you and hold your hand.
I promise to live as you'd want me to.
It's the only way now, to prove I loved you."

He put down the wild flowers he had brought,
And tenderly touched the bare earthen plot.
Then he squared his shoulders and searched the sky,
And he left—never knowing that I was nearby.

He returned in springtime, and as it would be, I
could see him, but he couldn't see me.
He stared, astonished at what he there found! The
flowers he'd brought had seeded the ground!

"Always Near By" continues . . .

Thick thistles and weed had grown all around,
But the flowers claimed every inch of the mound!
He had expected to find her plot bare,
And now, he knew, she had answered his prayer.

"This miracle speaks of your love and of peace!
From my guilt and my sorrow, it offers release.
I shall never forget you and all you have done!
I shall strive to be worthy of being your son."

He knelt at the grave-side and softly wept,
And kissed the ground where his mother slept,
Then squared his shoulders and smiled at the sky,
And he left—somehow knowing that I was near-by.

Folded Linens

Memories
Are like folded linens,
Stored
In the bureau of the mind,
Reviewed
From time to time
Until
Faded and crumbled
They dissolve
With the essence from whence
They came.

Acceptance

What folly to disbelieve
That which defies our rationale.
Our infantile mentality
Could think its way to Hell!

There is that which sharpest reason
Has no power to deny.
Wise the man who will accept,
And not attempt to reason why!

Somewhere

To those bereft of love affairs
(by circumstance betrayed)
And all those grieving without hope
For love that could not stay:

Once love exists it cannot be
Dissolved by time or space.
If you *will* it to continue,
It will exist—someplace.
Life has dreams and dreams have life!
The two thus intermix
In the somewhere of forever
Where righted wrongs exist,
Where lovers find fulfillment
And by *will* alone impart,
The aura and the force of love
Connecting heart to heart.

Until Then

Twenty-two years of caring
That ended in sorrow.
Twenty-two years of yesterdays
With no tomorrows.

Twenty-two years of memories
Tightly embraced!
Twenty-two years that fate
Abruptly erased.

Twenty-two years of blessings
Brought this curse.
Smiles around the cradle—
Tears around the hearse.

To accept what they can't change
Will be the hardest part.
Your dad and mom forever
Will hold you in their hearts.

Our faith in God assures us
That we will meet again.
Know, young man, without a doubt
They'll miss you, until then.

Reprimand

You lied to me.
You said,
"To know me better"
You pried from me
My secrets
And ambitions.
You extruded
My emotions
Like tooth paste
From a tube,
Then extracted
All the warmth
And exposed
My insecurity
To cold logic.
You expressed
Disgust,
Excusing,
As you must,
The tortuous routine—
You took my innocence
And made it guilt.
You lied to me.
You said,
"To know me better"
When all you wanted
Was to know
The worst.

Oh! conscience,
Why did you probe
So deep?

Lost

I walk
  on rocks.
    I fear
      too near
        the edge am I.

My mind
  holds time,
    like truth,
      too loose
        to recognize.

What was
  is not
    as I
      had thought.
        Not—anymore.

It seems
  I fell
    in this
      dark pond
        once before.

But just
  before
    I drowned
      I found
        a solid shore.

Is there
  any where
    the peace
      that I
        am searching for?

The Struggle

I will not cry!
Life, at best, is a struggling mind.
I will not cry.
This mess is a test for my struggling mind.
I will not cry.

I will think on pleasantries.
I will dwell on memories
Of smiles from another time.
I will sing up-beat
I will speak in rhyme
I will hide my sorrow.
I will wake tomorrow
And I will work
Like one possessed.
Who would have guessed
I could be so strong!

I will tell no one
That I cried last night,
All night long.

Exhausted!

I'm not Job, Lord!
I'm Joan.
I can't cut it
All alone!

I'm just too tired.
Can't get it done.
It's work for three, Lord!
Not for one.

I know You know.
I hate to gripe.
The day's too short.
So is the night.

There must be something
You can do
To help me, Lord!
It's up to You.

To Sleep

Yield to sleep.
Abandon thought.
Silent forces beckon
Ghosts that host
Intriguing rendezvous.

The summons, so proposed
No argument can contradict,
As by some sorcery transfixed,
Imposes will on will,
Luring listless consciousness
To misty regions that exist,
Of farce and logic, intermixed,
In the nowhere of the mind.

Yield to sleep.
Abandon thought.
Silent forces beckon
Ghosts that host
Intriguing rendezvous.

Optimistic Me!

"We can do it," I said.
as we caulked and scraped.
sealed the cracks, primed,
and sanded the wood.

"We can do it," I said.
as we dipped the brushes
and slopped the paint,
stretching as far as we could.

"We can do it," I said.
As the sun beat down
and our sweat soaked us wet,
through and through!

For three days straight
we did nothing by paint
until everything
sparkles like new.

"We did it!" I groaned,
"but never again!"
Exhausted,
I sank to the floor.

"They can do it," I said.
"Next time, I'll call
the professional painters
next door!"

On a Hot Afternoon

Green grasshoppers burping brown
Are all that's stirring in our town.
I lay in this old hammock, torn.
A book of verse, its pages worn
Is by my side but is not read.
It's much too hot to lift my head!

The dogs lay panting in the shade
While I sip sweet cold lemonade.
I should water, weed and hoe
But it's too hot to move, and so
The weeds within my garden thrive
While food plants struggle to survive.

The screens have need of mending, soon.
(A job for some cool afternoon.)
I think I hear the telephone.
I'll just pretend that I'm not home.
I wonder if my wife has made
Some more of this cold lemonade?

I wonder if she's found the time
To mend that favorite shirt of mine?
When her little chores are done,
Perhaps she'll take the time to run
Out to the mail box, just to see
If there is any mail for me.

"On a Hot Afternoon" continues . . .

It's good to lay beneath the trees!
The sun can't penetrate the leaves.
This stifling heat is hard to take!

I feel it more when I'm awake,
So I'll just doze here in the shade
And dream—of more—cold lem—o—nade

. . . ZZZZZZZZZZ

BY JOAN TENNER

More Like a Bird

I cannot by
Like Kilmer's tree
That stately stands
To grace the land
Through summer's heat
And Winter's frost,
To strip and change
(No modesty lost),
To remain a lifetime
Wherever seeded,
Providing shade
When it is needed,
Accepting rain,
Sharing the dew,
Catching the wind
As it swirls through!

I cannot be
Like Kilmer's tree,
Although the thought
Appeals to me.
I'd like to see
How it feels to be
Stationary,
To know everyone
And have them know me,
To stay in one place
Indefinitely.
I think about this
Quite often it seems,
But always uproot

"More Like a Bird" continues . . .

To a different scene,
Not by chance . . . .
By circumstance.
Each time I move
I take an oath,
"Never again!"
It seems I never
Can keep my word.
I'm not like a tree;
I'm more like a bird,
Nesting where I must
Not where I please.
Still, fate persists
In its shady tease
That someday I may
Find roots, like a tree.

The Couch is Mine!

Water
Trickling loudly,
Drop by drop.
Nothing
You can do, tonight,
Will make it stop.

Last week
You swore to me
That you could call
Someone
To come and fix
That waterfall!

Perhaps
The sheep
I'm counting
Should be fish!
Too bad
I can't plug leakage
With a wish!

Morning
Promises a plumber
To the scene.
For now,
Just pray that
I remain serene.

Echoes
Of the drops twit

"The Couch is Mine!" continues . . .

My addled mind.
Anger
Does inspire! The couch
I claim as mine!

If you
Should join me,
Close the door!
The couch
Is mine! You'll
Have the floor.

If this
Seems selfish, I
Apologize.
Last night
Lord knows, I
Hardly closed my eyes.

For worse
Or better, I
Have promised you,
But not
For leaking faucets
All night through!

A Hodgepodge

The paint on my canvas
Never gets dry.
I correct and change
So often that I
Alter the landscape
A hundred times,
From dismal to bright,
Adding few lines,
Subtracting a point
Of interest here,
And dabbing of splotch
Of color there.
Its' not at all what
It started to be!
It's hodgepodge of moods,
Just like me.

Neither Less – Nor More

They closed the brothel down in Deadwood
And put padlocks on the doors.
The whole town rocked with shock because
Their jail was full of whores.

The wives who never worried
When their guys went out at night,
Decided they'd stay close to home
And treat their husbands right!

Their evenings then, were taken up
Domestically and boring,
No longer free to browse and bridge
While husbands were out whoring.

It seemed the town was satisfied,
But some within were longing!
An auction help to post the bail
Sold all the whores' belongings.

The sheriff and his deputies
Had mixed emotions 'bout it.
The brothel came when sprang the town;
They'd never been without it.

It mattered not to all the guys!
Each said, "I've never been there"
The wives would never truly know
If their husbands ever went there.

"Neither Less – Nor More" continues . . .

Marriage vows all over town
Were strengthened and renewed.
Bachelors once more donned their best,
And single maids pursued

Let out of jail on auction bail,
The ladies soon were free.
They pried the padlock off the doors
And raised the standard fee.

Those of us most apt to judge
Should not blame a madam for
What is done with an accomplice,
Involved, neither less—nor more.

There's No Excuse

When someone speaks through spirits
And slurs his loud lament,
The problem is the arguer
And not the argument.

Louder, fouler come the words
With less and less the sense.
Unwittingly, the witless one
Commits a rude offense!

If you drink too much, don't argue!
Go quietly abed.
You will hate yourself for drinking,
But not for what you've said.

No one should have to suffer
A loud-mouthed drunk's abuse.
For such a breach of etiquette
There can be no excuse!

Double Trouble

The older I get, the more I forget
The things I should remember!
Not nursery rhymes or poetic lines
Nor songs of love, most tender.
But to pay what's due to the company
That keeps our light aglow,
And my husband's suits at the cleaners
And the names of people I know.
I forget where I put my glasses
And what I did with my rings
And where I hid my check book
And thousand other things.
I have talked to myself, (and listened)
And vowed to correct this condition.
I've tried every day, but forgetful I stay
And now, I've lost my ambition.
My husband tries to be patient
But says he has one regret:
The things that I always remember—
He wishes I would forget!

Bounty in Winter

Quite suddenly, it's Winter!
The blossom, green and seed . . . all spent.
Despite the chill, I am content.
(How swiftly softer seasons went!)

Though the hardships of this season
Come unbidden,
This wrinkled, barren world
Has bounty, hidden.
How kind, to find that memories
Thrive in Winter!

What's Next?

What will the next world
Hold for me?
How interesting
To suspect
Its dimensions,
Not in fear,
But in anticipation!
Personal Karma?
Reincarnation?
Heaven's reality
And finality
Are sure,
But in what frame?
How exciting, to be—
Knowing that once you are,
You are!

It's Time to Move-On

Discard this vessel
However you see fit.
I shall not be aware,
I shall not know or care.
I shall not be.
. . . no disappointments,
No desires, no demands
Of mind or hands!
All that was required of me
Has long ago been done.

I watch each setting sun
In muted awe!
I had all the best.
The struggle to reach
Each tomorrow
Seems so useless!

It's time to move on,
To dream new dreams.
I am old.

I have no promises to keep.
I welcome the eternal sleep!
Death is for the body
Not the soul.
Mortal man has never been
In full control.

So I pray to Thee,
"Set my spirit free!"

"It's Time to Move-On" continues . . .

Discard this vessel
However you see fit.
It is not me!
I shall not mind a bit.

The Face of Reality

"Her mind is gone," they say.
"She must be put away."
She confides in the stranger
Who always appears
To answer her questions
From deep in the mirror.
This wrinkled one
With wild gray hair,
Will stay, returning
Stare for stare
Or touch for touch
(though her flesh be cold,)
Unrecognized, unreal,
. . . unacceptably old.

BY JOAN TENNER

Prayer for Winnie

Most merciful Lord, please take her home.
She's old and confused and so alone!
She dreams, though awake, of yesterday.
Her family and friends have all passed away.

Her few lucid moments have proven to be
Less kind than her world of memory.
Between wheelchair and bed she exists, bodily.
Between childhood and death, suspended is she.

She does not see well, but she's looking for You.
She does not hear well, but she's listening, too.
She knows you are near, Lord, intuitively.
From her limbo of pain, she calls out to Thee.

Were I in her place, I would not want to stay.
She's ready to follow, if You'll lead the way.
She will not be dismayed, though the way be unknown.
She's waiting, dear Lord. Please take her home.

A Variable Constant

Though time is a constant,
To the child, it seems to crawl
Between birthdays and Christmas.

Teen years accelerate.
Time is wished over, and shoved
Toward life's fulfillment.

Adults strive to save time
As it seemingly passes
Faster and faster.

We pack each hour with more and more
Of whatever fills each day,
From rent to mortgage, pay to pay.

Later, with the children grown,
We have more time to call our own.
We stretch and try to slow it.

Old age arrives before we know it.
For some . . . in pain, in cloudy thought, in
Wretched loneliness . . . forgotten.

Time is a constant
But for such as these, the hours pass
Like chains through a tilted hourglass.

Each link stops before it drops.
The moment and the muddled mind . . .
Stuck in the bottleneck of time.

Prenatal, Again

They are silent within,
No longer aware
Of what has been,
As if to say, "What is to be
Will be without me."

They are silent within,
Existence lost
In oblivion,
As if to say, "I am not here,
Nor have I ever been."

Just once in a while
A familiar smile
Sparks recognition,
Seeming to say, "I knew you
But can't remember when."

Partially claimed, ancient,
They await what
They know not of,
As if, in exodus, prenatal
To hereafter like.

The Host

From the Greatest Physician,
This panacean bit of bread
Was prescribed for me
Before He died for me.
It makes me whole.
It heals my soul.
It makes me a part of
(attuned to the heart of)
His immortal plan
For weak and mortal man.

It is all I need.
Elixir, indeed!

The Leaving

She who strained to give me life
Now is strained to lose her own.
Each breath is a labor.
She attempts to find the way
Out of this existence
Into another day.

She is so close to finding out
What life was all about!

Come forth, you foregone spirits!
Mother, father, sisters, husband!
Come, claim this soul!
She has missed you all!
Who will come to call
This dear one to her rest?
She was the very best
Of temperate living!
She scans the horizon
Waiting for a guide
To show her the way
To the other side.
She is ready
For eternity!
She'll be so pleased to see
Every one of you!
Can't you hurry things along?
She needs to hear your strong
Command to let go of this struggle!
Please, speak to the Lord!
She awaits release.

"The Leaving" continues . . .

She has suffered enough!
God grant her peace!

I evoke you all
Give a helping hand
To that other land
Where she'll wait for me
And her progeny—forever.

Later:

What silence is this?
Something is missing!
Can she feel me kissing
Her toil worn hands?
Scant pulse—no breathing!
She is leaving!
She is sleeping away
Peacefully!

What does she see?
She has waited so long
For this moment to come.
Death must be Heaven
When the dying is done!
She had hoped
"It wouldn't take too long."
From the womb of earth
She is gone. She is gone!

Later:

I stare at the empty bed.
They have taken her away.
I do not wish her back.
She did not want to stay.

"The Leaving" continues . . .

Pain erodes the will.
She struggled until
Death seemed a better place.

I grieve, not because she's gone,
But that life must go on
Without her. Though I be sad,
It is time to give thanks
And spread the good news
About her! She is with Dad
In everlasting grace.

Now, she has found out
What life was all about!
Now, she found out
What God is all about!

In His time,
We shall meet again!

Joan Tenner

Joan Tenner began to write at an early age and continue throughout her life. Joan's poetry became her voice that expressed her ideas, her impressions and her reflections of her world beyond her kitchen window as she washed the dishes, cleaned her house and cared for her children.

Joan Tenner's writings were inspired, by Henry Wadsworth Longfellow who said, "Come read to me some . . . simple heartfelt lay to soothe restless feelings . . . Read from some humbler poet . . . "

So, Joan considered her poems as quite ordinary and simple writings;

She became the "Humbler Poet!"

She has authored two volumes of poetry . . . This her first book Consider the Humbler Poet and a second book entitled Journey Through Thistles and Time. A third in the series will be available in 2024 from Wisdom House Books entitled A Collection from the Humbler Poet.

Joan's Halloween stories, entitled Grandma's Halloween Stories were written between 1989 through 1996 for her grandchildren and were published by Wisdom House Books in 2020.

All her books are available at www.thehumblerpoet.com